Introduction to T Providers

by

Deepak Vohra

Foreword

With the advent of the Internet and the World Wide Web (WWW) came the challenge of how different computer systems and applications are to interact with each other. For information and resources to be exchanged over the web, applications can expose an Application Programming Interface (API) using the Representational State Transfer (REST) software architecture or model. Clients who want to access these resources can do so with a client tool using the REST API endpoints exposed by the applications.

What This Book Covers?

The book introduces Terraform Providers as objects that can manage resources exposed by RESTful APIs.

What You Need for This Book?

The book requires some knowledge of RESTful API services, and the Golang.

Who is This Book For?

The primary target audience of the book is web application developers.

Source Code

The source code for the example Terraform provider is available on the GitHub at https://github.com/Deepak-Vohra/terraform and https://github.com/Deepak-Vohra/terraform-provider-example.

Table Of Contents

1 Introduction.   1

1.1 Terraform Providers.   1

1.2 Benefits.   1

1.3 The Terraform Configuration Language.   1

1.4. Advantages Over a Web Console.   2

1.5 The Example REST API.   2

1.6 Sequence of Phases.   2

1.7 Summary.   3

2 What are Terraform Providers?.   5

2.1 Components.   5

2.2 Basic Structure of a Terraform Provider.   6

2.3 Schema Definition for Resources and Attributes.   7

2.4 Data Sources for Retrieving Information.   8

2.5 Resource Lifecycle Management Functions.   8

2.6 Summary.   10

3 Authentication and API Interaction.   11

3.1 Creating an Account and a Project.   11

3.2 Uploading an SSH Key.   16

3.3 Getting an API Token.   20

3.4 Getting an API Endpoint.   21

3.5 Summary.   23

4 Developing a Terraform Provider.   25

4.1 Provider Development Approaches.   25

4.2 Prerequisite Setup.   25

4.3 Initializing a Golang Module.   26

4.4 Creating a Terraform Provider Schema.   26

4.5 Creating a Provider Entrypoint.   27

4.6 Creating a Resource Schema.   28

4.7 Configuring the go-resty Client.   29

4.8 Creating Resource Action Functions.   30

    4.8.1 Create Functionality.   32

    4.8.2 Read Functionality.   34

    4.8.3 Update Functionality.   34

    4.8.4 Delete Functionality.   35

4.9 Error handling and logging.   35

4.10 Compiling the Golang Source Code to Binaries. 40

4.11 Summary.   41

5. Terraform CLI.   43

5.1 Configuring Terraform CLI.   43

5.2 Creating Terraform Configuration Files.   43

5.3 Using Terraform CLI.   45

5.4 Summary.   50

6. Terraform Provider Best Practices.   51

6.1 Development.   51

6.2 Style & Structure.   52

6.3 Testing and Hosting.   53

6.4 Documentation.   54

6.5 Security.   54

6.6 Versioning & Publishing.   56

6.7 Summary.   56

7. Afterword.   57

INDEX.   59

1 Introduction

In this chapter, we will cover the following topics:

- Introduce Terraform Providers
- Introduce the benefits of Terraform Providers
- Introduce Terraform Configuration Language
- Introduce advantages over a web console
- Introduce an example REST API
- Describe the sequence of development phases

First, we introduce Terraform Providers.

1.1 Terraform Providers

Terraform Providers are plugins to manage resources as code, an approach more commonly known as Infrastructure as Code (IaC). The resources are objects from kind of managed services. The resources that Terraform Providers manage do not have to be physical infrastructure resources such as VM Compute instances, or network VPCs. The resources can be IaaS (Infrastructure as a Service) PaaS (Platform as a Service) resources or SaaS (Software as a Service) resources. Terraform Providers can manage resources that expose RESTful API endpoints.

1.2 Benefits

We need to use providers in scenarios where we are using the IaC approach to manage our infrastructure. There are several benefits from using providers for managing our resources:

- Automation
- Flexibility
- Ease of infrastructure management
- Integration with CI/CD Pipelines
- Collaboration
- Support for policy-as-code (PAC) frameworks

1.3 The Terraform Configuration Language

We use a Terraform Provider when we want to manage REST API operations with the Terraform Configuration Language. The configuration language lets us describe infrastructure objects as Terraform resources declaratively. We can describe, completely, in Terraform configuration, what infrastructure resources we want to manage, and how we want to manage them. How do Terraform Providers fit in with the Terraform configuration language? A Terraform Provider provides CRUD (Create, Read, Update, Delete) functionality to manage real infrastructure resources. We configure Terraform Providers that we develop or sourced from a registry in our Terraform configuration, and the Terraform configuration takes care of the rest. Based on the configuration, Terraform knows whether to create a new infrastructure resource instance, update it, or delete it.

1.4. Advantages Over a Web Console

We could log into a web console for the same resources and manage resources just as well, but a Terraform Provider is better aligned with Agile software development and the DevOps' principles. By managing infrastructure/resources as code, we can share the resources far more easily than using the web console details of resources. We can reuse the same codebase to spin up new resources. We can respond to change quickly by changing the codebase for a Provider directly instead of logging into a web console to perform modifications by clicking on the Modify/Update button and specifying new values. We can automate the process of creating/updating/deleting resources when we use a Terraform Provider. We can integrate Terraform Providers into CI/CD pipelines. We can use policy-as-code (PAC) frameworks to define and apply fine-grained, logic-based policies.

1.5 The Example REST API

In this short book, we will show how to create a custom Terraform provider to integrate a REST API into our existing Terraform-based infrastructure. We may already be familiar with Terraform and want to integrate REST API resources into our existing infrastructure as code (IaC) workflow.

We shall use Platform.sh as an example REST API for developing a Terraform Provider. Platform.sh is a PaaS (Platform as a Service), and therefore the provider we build provides a PaaS resource - Environment, for example. Platform.sh API does not expose any endpoints for physical infrastructure resources such as VMs. Platform.sh provides API endpoints for organizations, projects, environments, git repositories, source code operations, runtime operations, and deployments.

This provider we shall develop is built using a dummy host address. In real-world use, you would host your provider on a web host, and publish your provider to a registry such as the Terraform Registry (https://registry.terraform.io/) so that others can use it.

1.6 Sequence of Phases

This short book defines a Terraform provider, explores its structure, develops an example provider, and concludes with best practices. In the sequence illustrated for provider end use in Figure 1.1, you'll learn about step 1.

Figure 1.1 Sequence of phases to build and use a provider

1.7 Summary

In this chapter we introduced Terraform providers, and its relation to the Terraform Configuration Language. We briefly went over its benefits. We introduced the example REST API (Platform.sh) that we shall use to develop an example Terraform provider. Finally, we described the sequence of phases in the development of a Terraform provider, and how this short book fits into it.

In the next chapter we describe a Terraform provider in more detail.

2 What Are Terraform Providers?

In this chapter, we will cover the following topics:

- Components of a Terraform Provider
- Structure of a Terraform Provider
- Resource Schemas
- Data Sources
- Resource Lifecycle

First, we introduce the different components of a Terraform Provider.

2.1 Components

Terraform providers are plugins used to automate infrastructure to create and manage resources, typically resources on the cloud. Real-world resources are exposed by different vendor REST APIs such as AWS, and Platform.sh. Terraform Providers are logical abstractions of the APIs to provide them to end users as Terraform resources. More precisely, the REST APIs expose them as Golang software that can be used to interact with the APIs. A Provider is the software that abstracts RESTful API resources, and Terraform manages the resources based on a set of configurations that you use. We can declare resources and providers in configuration files and use a Terraform command line interface (CLI) to install and manage the resources. We don't have to use all the resources provided by a provider. We can configure only the resource/s we need to manage in the configuration file/s. The term "resource" can be used in two contexts: the real-world infrastructure resource, and the Terraform resource that abstracts the infrastructure resource.

Terraform has two logical components: **Terraform Core** and **Terraform Plugins**. Terraform Core is a compiled binary that is available through the Terraform command line interface (CLI). We can use the Terraform CLI to initialize, validate, plan, and apply the Terraform configuration described within one or more configuration files in a working directory. The Terraform CLI does all the dredge work including provider discovery and installation. The Terraform Plugins constitute the functionality that we may want to use with Terraform. Terraform Providers are nothing but Terraform Plugins. Another type of plugins is called Provisioners. Provisioners may optionally be used to perform associated actions for a resource such as pass data and create configuration files. The Terraform CLI invokes the Terraform providers over RPC (Remote procedure call). Figure 2.1 illustrates Terraform Providers as Golang binaries that interact with REST APIs, and Terraform CLI as a client that interacts with the providers.

Figure 2.1. Terraform Providers interaction with Terraform CLI and REST APIs

2.2 Basic Structure of a Terraform Provider

Terraform providers are based on the Terraform plugins architecture. If we want to build custom resource providers, Terraform recommends using the schema package instead of the core Terraform API because the former provides a high-level interface.

A Terraform Provider is Golang software. The software is developed as Go modules - a module is a collection of Go packages with a go.mod file, which describes the module path and the dependencies. A provider has the following functionality:

- Define Resources and data sources that map to real-word infrastructure services
- Authenticate with the infrastructure services (IaaS, PaaS, SaaS)
- Make calls to the infrastructure REST API endpoints
- Provide logic/functionality (CRUD) to manage the infrastructure resource/s
- Provide logic to save the resource's current state in a cached state file

A Terraform Provider must use one of the SDKs for Providers:

- Terraform Plugin SDK
- Terraform Plugin SDK v2
- Terraform Plugin Framework

We have used the Terraform Plugin SDK v2 in this short book as it has been tested in production extensively with most existing providers making use of it. The Terraform Plugin Framework is said to offer some benefits, and can always be migrated to if so preferred. Terraform follows the Write>Plan>Apply paradigm in infrastructure automation. The Plan phase is important because creating or making changes to real-world infrastructure must be reviewed before actually applying.

A provider is based on two data structures : *schemas* and *resources*. A schema describes the structure and type information of a value. Schemas are fundamental to defining any resource. Schema is a high-level framework for writing new Terraform providers.

6

Schema breaks down provider creation into simple create, read, update and delete operations for resources. The logic of whether to update, create, delete, etc. is all handled by the framework. The plugin developer does need to implement a configuration schema and the logic for CRUD operations.

A resource schema defines attributes that are mapped to real-world resources. As an example you could define a Provider resource called `example_server` with resource attributes `environment_id` and `name`. The `environment_id` could map to the `environmentId` for an AWS, or other, REST API. The term "resources" is used to refer to two different concepts. One is the resource that is real-world managed service objects such as a virtual machine, a network VPC, or a PaaS project. The other is Terraform resource described with Terraform Plugin SDK V2 and Terraform Configuration Language. Terraform resources map to real-world resources. One provider can manage one or more infrastructure resources, which can be top-level or nested within other resources.

A Terraform module is a self-contained collection of Terraform configurations that are used together. A Terraform provider is an abstraction of a REST API that exposes infrastructure resources. Terraform Registry hosts both Terraform providers, and Terraform modules.

2.3 Schema Definition for Resources and Attributes

Terraform provider resources are defined using schemas. A schema for any resource is a collection of attributes and additional details describing the attribute's behavior such as its type, its default value, whether it is optional or required, whether it is computed. A required attribute must always be user specified in configuration and cannot be computed. An `id` attribute is implicitly added for each resource as its unique identifier, and its value is known only after the apply operation; after an infrastructure resource is changed. An attribute's `Type` field must always be set because we will use it to get a resource's data and whether it is a new configuration in Terraform along with the state of the resource saved by Terraform, or the plan for a resource. We need the type both to get data from the plan and to set the resource's data in state. Type is the type of the value and must be one of the following data types:

- TypeBool
- TypeInt
- TypeFloat
- TypeString
- TypeList
- TypeMap
- TypeSet

Resources can be top-level or nested within other resources. The Resource abstraction in Terraform can represent any of the following:

- Managed Resource
- Data Resource or Data Source
- Block

This short book discusses developing a provider for a managed resource with REST API endpoints to initialize, update, read and delete.

2.4 Data Sources for Retrieving Information

A provider can use data sources to retrieve some meta information that you can use in some resource. The data can come from outside of Terraform, from another Terraform configuration, or from a function. Typically, we would use a data source to read some information and use it in some resource. Data sources are also resources with an associated schema in Terraform but with the difference that they only support the read lifecycle operation. Data sources don't have a full CRUD functionality. Resource instances for data sources must have a Read function and must not implement Create, Update or Delete. Data sources are not saved in state and are always built completely from scratch on each read. Whereas a resource is declared in Terraform configuration with the resource {} block, a data source is declared with the data {} block. Some examples of data sources in the aws provider are aws_launch_template to get information about a Launch Template, and aws_instance to get the ID of an Amazon EC2 Instance.

```
data "aws_launch_template" "default" {
  name = "my-launch-template"
}
```

Data sources are used to get meta data that can be used in other provider resources.

2.5 Resource Lifecycle Management Functions

A resource that is managed by Terraform uses the built-in resource lifecycle management functionality for create, read, update, and delete operations on infrastructure resources. We only need to implement the CRUD functions and Terraform determines on its own which function to call based on the configuration provided when we apply it. Teraform Plugin SDK v2 provides three variants each for the create, read, update, and delete resource life cycle operations. For the create functionality the resource lifecycle functions are Create, CreateContext, and CreateWithoutTimeout in the schema package. Only one of Create, CreateContext, or CreateWithoutTimeout should be implemented. Similarly, three variants each are supported for read, update, and delete. The functions with the `Context` suffix are context aware, and their function parameter list includes a `Context` parameter that can be used to store SDK information such as loggers and timeouts. The `Context`-suffixed functions have a timeout associated with them with a default setting of 20 minutes. We can customize timeouts with the `Timeouts` field or we can use functions suffixed `WithoutTimeout` such as `CreateWithoutTimeout` that have no timeouts. Terraform plugin SDK v2 recommends to use the `Context`-suffixed functions.

The resource lifecycle of a managed resource is illustrated in Figure 2.2.

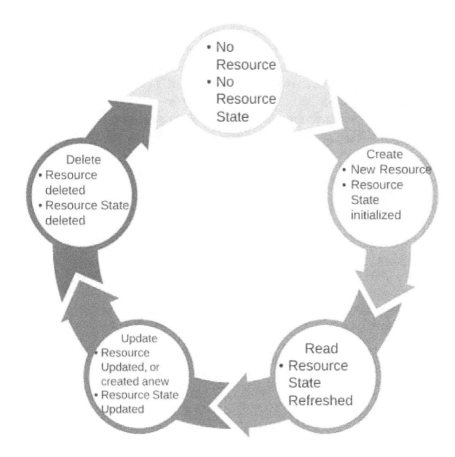

Figure 2.2 Resource Lifecycle for a Managed Resource

A provider developer must code the logic for the CRUD functionality in the respective function implementations. A developer must also code the logic for saving a resource's state in the cached state file. What the Terraform framework does is to call the right function with a given Terraform configuration.

Terraform maintains/caches the current state of the resource at all times in a file `terraform.tfstate`. The state is mapped to real-world resources. There is a one-to-one mapping between remote objects and their records in the state. The terraform state can be refreshed explicitly by calling `terraform refresh`, which is usually not needed. Terraform automatically refreshes the state of the resources it keeps by syncing with actual resources each time the `terraform plan`, or `terraform apply` is called. But because the resource state syncing could involve some extra bandwidth auto refresh can be turned off. Terraform reliably caches the current state regardless of periodic refresh/sync - auto or explicit, after each `terraform apply`. The `terraform show` command can be used to print state.

It is imperative that we manage resources with Terraform only. Terraform does not automatically update a resource's state that it keeps if we were to go outside Terraform framework and change the resources, such as by direct login to the web console. Changing Terraform managed resources directly, outside of Terraform, introduces drift. Terraform CLI provides some command options if we want to sync our state file with the infrastructure resources after directly changing the resources. We can use the `terraform plan -refresh-only`, and `terraform apply -refresh-only` commands to sync Terraform state. These two commands without the `-refresh-only` mode do an in-memory sync of state with infrastructure state each time they are used before making any recommendations or changes.

2.6 Summary

In this chapter we discussed the different components of Terraform providers, and how Terraform providers interact with REST API resources. We discussed the basic structure, and functionality of a Terraform Provider software. We introduced how Terraform resources are defined using schemas. Terraform providers can use data sources for external data. We concluded the chapter by discussing the resource lifecycle management for a Terraform managed resource.

A Terraform Provider is responsible for the authentication and API interaction with the cloud resources that it manages, for example Platform.sh. In the next chapter we discuss authentication and resource API interaction in a Terraform provider. As discussed in the next chapter, we need to create an API Token that can be used to create OAuth2 Access Tokens that a provider can use to authenticate.

3 Authentication and API Interaction

In this chapter, we will cover authentication and API interaction.

Note: The authentication information is likely to be different for different REST APIs. However, the procedure would be similar, one that involves getting an authentication key, or token.

3.1 Creating an Account and a Project

A Terraform Provider does the authentication and API interaction with the example Platform.sh. We need to set up a Platform.sh account and create an organization, project and environment at the least. We need to do this because we need an API endpoint to make REST API calls. We also need to create an API Token, which can be used to create OAuth2 Access Tokens. Login and create your first project. Click on **Create project** as shown in Figure 3.1.

Figure 3.1. Create project

In the dialog prompt to create an organization click on **Create organization**. as shown in Figure 3.2.

11

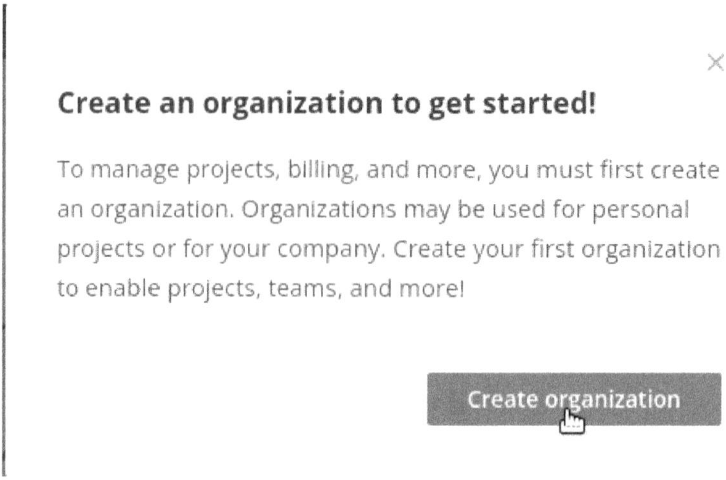

Create an organization to get started!

To manage projects, billing, and more, you must first create an organization. Organizations may be used for personal projects or for your company. Create your first organization to enable projects, teams, and more!

Create organization

Figure 3.2. Create organization

An organization gets created as shown in Figure 3.3.

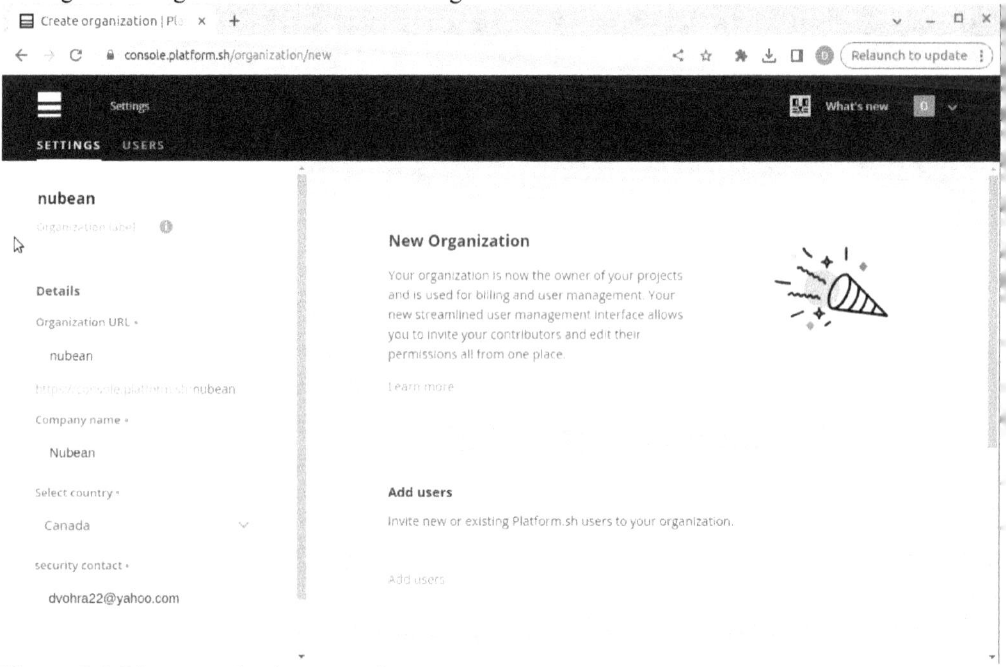

Figure 3.3. New organization created

Select **All projects** from the drop-down as shown in Figure 3.4.

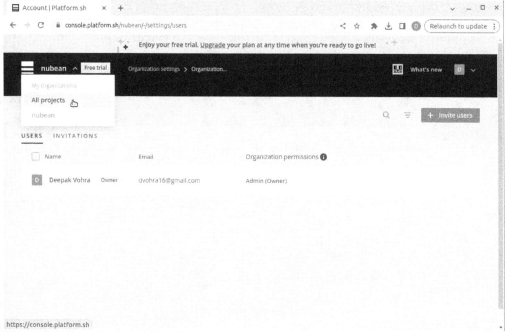

Figure 3.4. Organization>All projects

Click on **Create project** to create a project as shown in Figure 3.5.

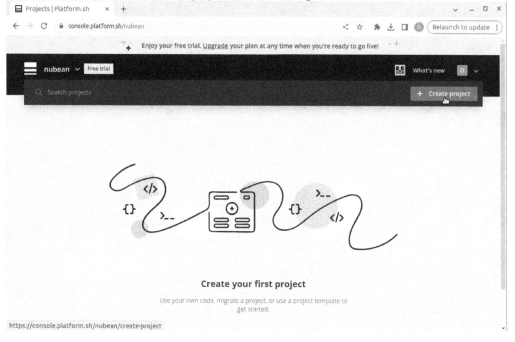

Figure 3.5. Create project

In **New project** sub-window select project type. Click on **Use a template** as shown in Figure 3.6.

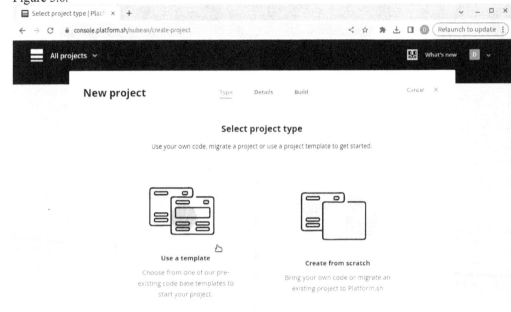

Figure 3.6. Use a template

Select a template (Express.js as an example) as shown in Figure 3.7.

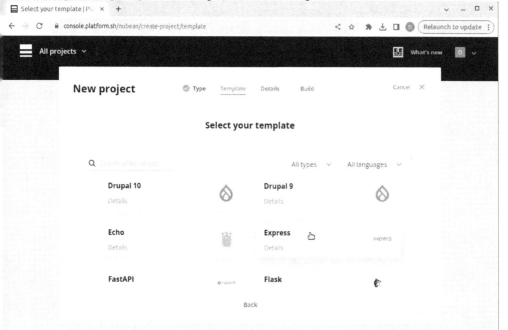

Figure 3.7. Selecting Express.js template

Specify project details and click on **Create project** as shown in Figure 3.8.

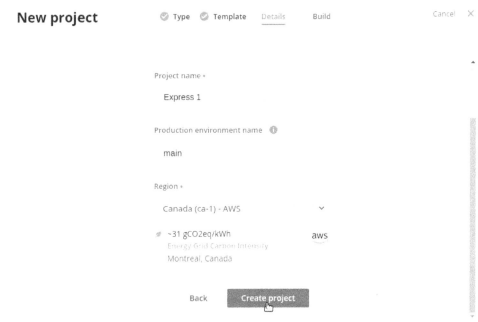

Figure 3.8. Project details

The Development plan is the lowest level plan, which includes a 30-day trial. Click on **Continue**. A new project gets created as shown in Figure 3.9.

Figure 3.9. An Express.js based project

The new project has only one environment (**Main** by default). The source code can be cloned using the **git clone** command listed in Figure 3.10.

3.2 Uploading an SSH Key

You need to upload your SSH Key to Platform.sh to be able to access the codebase.

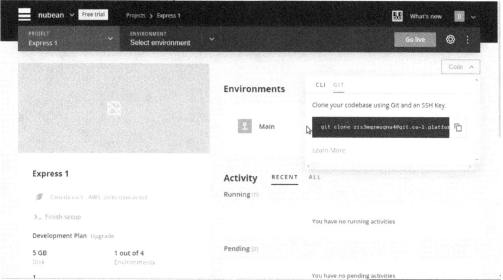

Figure 3.10. Git URL for Project Codebase

Select **SSH Keys> Add public key** as shown in Figure 3.11 to add a SSH key that you created on your local machine with ssh-keygen.

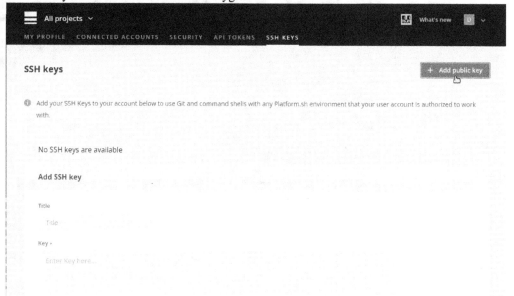

Figure 3.11. Add public key

Copy and paste the key in the **Key** text field and click on **Save**. as shown in Figure 3.12.

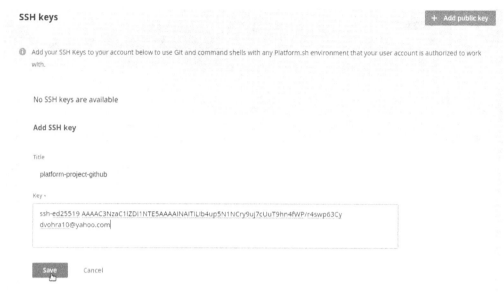

Figure 3.12. Adding Key

A new key gets added as shown in Figure 3.13.

Figure 3.13. New key added

The project id for a project can be obtained from the console as shown in Figure 3.14.

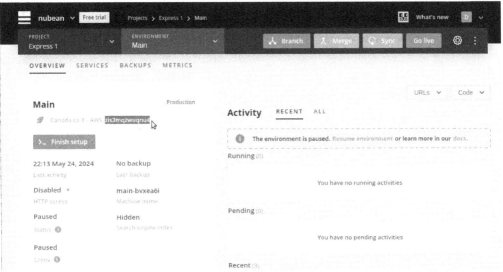

Figure 3.14. Project id

If you want to create a branch environment, click on **Branch** as shown in Figure 3.15.

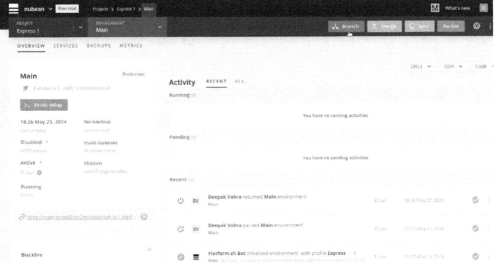

Figure 3.15. Creating a Branch environment

Two environments are listed as shown in Figure 3.16.

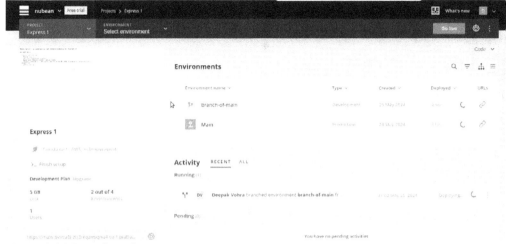

Figure 3.16. Branch environment

3.3 Getting an API Token

To create an API Token, select My Profile from your account icon. Select the **API Tokens** tab. Click on **Create API Token** as shown in Figure 3.17.

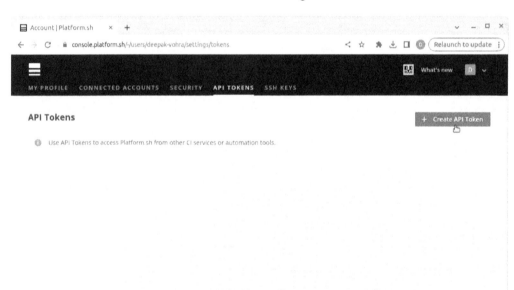

Figure 3.17. API Tokens>Create API Token

Specify a name and click on **Create API Token** as shown in Figure 3.18.

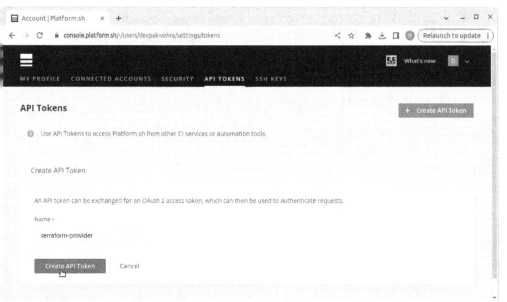

Figure 3.18. Specifying API Token Name

An API Token gets created. Click on **Copy** as shown in Figure 3.19 to copy the token and store it in a file. You won't be able to find the API Token later if you lose the copy you have stored.

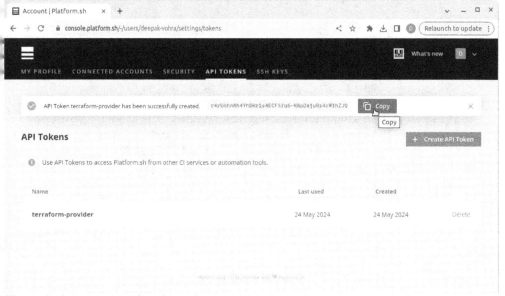

Figure 3.19. New API Token Created

3.4 Getting an API Endpoint

To obtain a temporary-use access token, run the following command with `API_TOKEN` placeholder replaced with the actual API Token copied in the previous screen.

```
curl -u platform-api-user: \
    -d 'grant_type=api_token&api_token=API_TOKEN' \
    https://auth.api.platform.sh/oauth2/token
```

The output JSON includes an `access_token` field. Copy the `access_token` string.

```
user@localhost:~$ curl -u platform-api-user: \
>       -d
'grant_type=api_token&api_token=r4rUhhnNh4YhDHr1s4ECFSfq6-
N8pDajuRz4cWfhZJQ' \
>       https://auth.api.platform.sh/oauth2/token
{"access_token":"eyJhbGciOiJee","expires_in":899,"scope":""
,"token_type":"bearer"}
```

Copy the `access_token` string. The access token can be used to access Platform.sh resources such as projects and environments. To list all projects, run the curl command:

```
curl -H "Authorization: Bearer eyJhbGciOiJFUzI1NiIsImtpZC "
\
    https://api.platform.sh/projects
```

The output lists the project we created earlier in the web console.

```
{"count":1,"projects":[{"id":"zis3mqzwuqnu4","endpoint":"ht
tps:\/\/ca-
1.platform.sh\/api\/projects\/zis3mqzwuqnu4","ui":"https:\/
\/console.platform.sh\/01hypmrnb9fnz24twv2mr5adqg\/zis3mqzw
uqnu4","subscription_id":"2","owner":"01HYPMRNB","owner_inf
o":{"type":"organization"},"organization_id":"01HYPMRNB9FN"
,"_links":{"self":{"href":"https:\/\/accounts.platform.sh\/
api\/v1\/subscriptions\/294"}}}],"_links":{"self":{"title":
"Self","href":"https:\/\/accounts.platform.sh\/api\/v1\/sub
scriptions"},"ref:organizations:0":{"href":"\/ref\/organiza
tions?in=01HYPMR"}}}
```

The `endpoint` attribute lists the API endpoint for the project as https://ca-1.platform.sh/api/projects/zisqnu after removing the "\" used as escape character. Similarly, all the environments for a given project can be listed with command:

```
user@localhost:~/terraform-provider-example$ curl -H
"Authorization: Bearer eyJhbGciOiJFUzI1NiIsI" \
>
https://api.platform.sh/projects/zis3mqzwuqnu4/environments
```

The output JSON object lists all the environments with the
main project as the first.

```
[
  {
    "id": "main",
    "_links": {
      "self": {
        "href": "https://ca-
1.platform.sh/api/projects/zis3mqzwuqnu4/environments/main"
      },
      "#edit": {
        "href":
"/api/projects/zis3mqzwuqnu4/environments/main"
      },
...
    "has_code": true,
    "head_commit":
"2b6b24e262dddf5ffb32ec73081d9c63e839e06e",
    "merge_info": {
      "commits_ahead": 0,
      "commits_behind": 0,
      "parent_ref": null
    },
    "has_deployment": true
  }
]
```

We can use the API endpoints and resource Id thus obtained in your resource API calls in the provider, as we discuss later.

3.5 Summary

In this chapter we introduced authentication, and how to obtain an API endpoint.

In the next chapter we describe a Terraform provider in more detail.

4 Developing a Terraform Provider

In this chapter, we will cover the following topics:

- Provider Development Approaches
- Prerequisite Setup
- Initializing a Golang Module
- Creating a Terraform Provider Schema
- Creating a Resource Schema
- Configuring the go-resty Client
- Creating Resource Action Functions
- Error Handling and Logging
- Compiling the Golang Source Code to Binaries

First, we introduce the different approaches to developing a Terraform Provider.

4.1 Provider Development Approaches

The Golang-HashiCorp Configuration Language combination has become the de facto standard for resource provider development. Terraform providers interact with all kinds of cloud services (IaaS, SaaS,PaaS). Some other options for Infrastructure as Code are available such AWS CloudFormation. CloudFormation initially supported only AWS resources but recently has started to support third-party resources (https://aws.amazon.com/blogs/devops/extending-cloudformation-and-cdk-with-third-party-extensions/) . CloudFormation makes use of its own resource specification (https://docs.aws.amazon.com/AWSCloudFormation/latest/UserGuide/cfn-resource-specification-format.html) . Some similarity in resource declaration/specification does exist such as that both HashiCorp Configuration Language and AWS CloudFormation resource specification based resources can be described in JSON. Terraform and Providers are different technologies in general. We can develop a Terraform provider that has a dependency on a third-party provider, perhaps not developed with Terraform plugin SDK. Some other third-party options for developing custom resource providers include Puppet Development Kit(PDK) with the Resource API, and CloudFormation Command Line Interface (CFN-CLI). The CloudFormation CLI is an open source project to define and create resource providers.

4.2 Prerequisite Setup

As a prerequisite setup, install Golang (https://go.dev/doc/install) and Terraform (https://developer.hashicorp.com/terraform/install). To be able to use the latest features install the latest stable version of each. The golang version can be found with the go version command, and the Terraform version can be found with the `terraform version` command. Two Terraform directories are of interest. The `~/.terraform.d/plugins` directory is from where Terraform finds providers installed locally. The `terraform init` command downloads and installs any required dependency providers in this directory. The `~/.terraform.d/plugin-cache` is used to cache plugin/provider binaries. When updating and recompiling binaries during development, remember to delete the old binaries from the `~/.terraform.d/plugin-cache`. The procedure to build a provider involves the sequence of coding tasks shown in Figure 4.1.

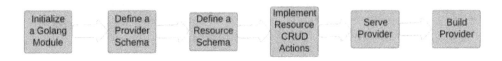

Figure 4.1. Sequence to build a Provider

4.3 Initializing a Golang Module

Create a directory for the Provider's Golang source code. Change the current directory to the new directory.

```
$ mkdir ~/terraform-provider-example
$ cd ~/terraform-provider-example
```

Initialize a new module with `go mod init` command. Outside GOPATH , module path for source directory must be specified. :

```
~/terraform-provider-example$ go mod init
example.com/terraform-provider-example
```

The output is:

```
go: creating new go.mod: module example.com/terraform-
provider-example
```

A Golang module gets created. Initially, the only file in the directory is go.mod.

```
:~/terraform-provider-example$ ls -l -rw-rw-r-- 1
deepakvohra deepakvohra 57 May 25 22:49 go.mod
```

The go.mod file lists the module path and the version.

4.4 Creating a Terraform Provider Schema

If you want to build custom resource providers, Terraform recommends using the schema package, which breaks down provider creation into simple create, read, update and delete operations for resources. The logic of whether to update, create, delete, etc. is all handled by the framework. The plugin developer *does* need to implement a configuration schema and the logic for CRUD operations.

Define the provider schema for a simple Platform.sh resource (e.g., Environment). In the ~/terraform-provider-example directory for which we initialized a Golang module, create a source code file provider.go to add the Provider() function. Go's modular packaging provides flexibility regarding file naming, file size, and number of files in a package. We can change the names of any of the source code files, or the Terraform configuration files as there is no file name binding to functionality. All source code is created in the same package.

Provider represents a resource provider in Terraform. Resource, for our example provider, is an abstraction for a Terraform managed resource. A managed resource is an infrastructure component with a schema, and lifecycle operations such as create, read, update, and delete. Define the provider structure with the schema.Provider struct. ResourcesMap is the mapping of available resources that this provider can manage to their respective schemas. A schema is a schema.Resource struct along with their Resource structure defining their own schemas and CRUD operations. Provider automatically handles routing operations such as Apply to the proper resource. To fully implement managed resources, the Provider type ResourcesMap field should include a reference to an implementation of this type. In the example Provider the resource name is example_server and it must be specified in double quotes as a string. It is mapped to a function resourceServer() that returns a schema.Resource.

```go
// provider.go
package main

import (
    "github.com/hashicorp/terraform-plugin-sdk/v2/helper/schema"
)

func Provider() *schema.Provider {
    return &schema.Provider{
        ResourcesMap: map[string]*schema.Resource{
            "example_server": resourceServer(),
        },
    }
}
```

27

The `example_server` key is used later in Terraform configuration's resource directive to declare the resource you want to manage with Terraform.

4.5 Creating a Provider Entrypoint

Create a second source code file in the same package to serve the provider, or the entry point for the provider. The `plugin.Serve` function serves the provider. This function never returns and should be the final function called in the `main` function of the provider plugin. The `main()` function calls the `Provider()` function that is specified in the `provider.go` file. The `terraform-platform-plugin.go` file is listed:

```go
package main

import (

    "github.com/hashicorp/terraform-plugin-
sdk/v2/helper/schema"

    "github.com/hashicorp/terraform-plugin-sdk/v2/plugin"

)

func main() {

    plugin.Serve(&plugin.ServeOpts{

        ProviderFunc: func() *schema.Provider {

            return Provider()

        },

    })

}
```

4.6 Creating a Resource Schema

In the `provider.go` file the resource is mapped to a function `resourceServer()` that returns a `schema.Resource`. Next, we define the `resourceServer()` function. Create a third file `resource_server.go` for all resource related code. The only requirement for managing a resource is to use the `schema.Resource` type to define the data schema and the create, read, update, and delete actions/functions mapping. All four actions create, read, update, and delete and the corresponding functions must be specified. The `schema.Resource` struct includes:

- Fields for resource lifecycle functions such as `CreateContext`, `ReadContext`, `UpdateContext`, and `DeleteContext`
- A `Schema` field to define resource attributes

The `schema.Schema` mapping specifies the required and optional attributes. A required attribute must be provided in the Terraform configuration when using the Terraform CLI to call the Provider binaries or an error message will be output. We have defined two resource attributes, `environment_id`, and `name`, of which only the first is required. An `id` attribute is implicitly added for each resource as its unique identifier. An attribute's `Type` field must always be set because we need it both to get data from the plan, and to set the resource's data in state. Schema describes the structure and type information of a value. Schema is used in Provider and Resource types for managed resources and is fundamental to the implementations of `ResourceData`.

```
func resourceServer() *schema.Resource {
    return &schema.Resource{
        CreateContext: resourceServerCreate,
        ReadContext: resourceServerRead,
        UpdateContext: resourceServerUpdate,
        DeleteContext: resourceServerDelete,

        Schema: map[string]*schema.Schema{
            "environment_id": &schema.Schema{
                Type: schema.TypeString,
                Required: true,
            },
            "name": &schema.Schema{
                Type: schema.TypeString,
                Optional: true,
                Default: "a platform env",
            },
        },
    }
}
```

The `Type` determines what type is expected/valid in configuring an attribute's value. The `Type` also determines what type is returned when `ResourceData.Get` is called. The mapping between `Type` and the return value's type is relisted:

```
TypeBool - bool
TypeInt - int
TypeFloat - float64
TypeString - string
TypeList - []interface{}
TypeMap - map[string]interface{}
```

How does Terraform determine which provider functionality to call? Terraform gets the resource data changes to apply from the resources' configuration in Terraform configuration files. Terraform does this when the terraform plan is called to build a plan. Terraform automatically determines and calls the appropriate provider function by comparing the Terraform configuration for the resource and the current state of the resource to apply the plan when the `terraform apply` command is run.

4.7 Configuring the go-resty Client

Platform.sh API provides HTTP endpoints for the CRUD operations. Use the go-resty library to make HTTP calls to Platform.sh API endpoints. Before implementing the CRUD functions, get familiar with the go-resty library. It can be imported by including `"github.com/go-resty/resty/v2"` in the `import` block. Create a new instance of the client as follows:

```
client := resty.New()
```

The go-resty client provides Get, Put, Post, Patch, and Delete functions to call HTTP endpoints. Platform.sh API provides HTTP endpoints for most of the CRUD operations. Platform.sh does not provide an API endpoint for creating a new environment from scratch, but it does provide an endpoint for initializing a new environment off an existing environment with the provision to use a new Git repository for the new environment. How the different go-resty functions map to the different Platform.sh endpoint operations is illustrated in Figure 4.2.

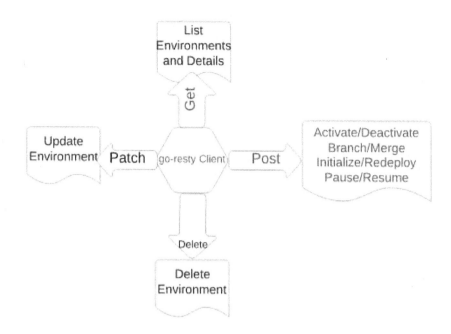

Figure 4.2. Go-resty Functions Map to Platform.sh API

4.8 Creating Resource Action Functions

The four CRUD functions must be implemented by the developer to build a custom provider as follows:

- Create - Define the logic to create the IaaS/PaaS/SaaS resource and set its Terraform state
- Read - Define the logic to refresh the Terraform state for the resource
- Update - Define the logic to update the IaaS/PaaS/SaaS resource and set/refresh the updated Terraform state on success
- Delete - Define the logic to delete the resource and remove the Terraform state on success

The majority of the coding requirement in developing a custom Terraform provider is in creating the resource CRUD functions. We shall get you started by providing some basic templates for these functions. The precise logic would depend on what resource you want to manage, and how you want to manage it. The function names must be the same as specified in the schema.Resource mapping . The function parameter list is based on whether you specified Create, CreateContext, or CreateWithoutTimeout (similarly for read, update, and delete) in the schema.Resource. The four functions without any logic are as follows:

```go
func resourceServerCreate(ctx context.Context, d *
schema.ResourceData, m interface {}) diag.Diagnostics {

    //implementation logic
    d.SetId("a unique resource id")
    return resourceServerRead(d, m)

}

func resourceServerRead(ctx context.Context, d *
schema.ResourceData, m interface {}) diag.Diagnostics {

    //implementation logic
    return nil
}

func resourceServerUpdate(ctx context.Context, d *
schema.ResourceData, m interface {}) diag.Diagnostics {

    //implementation logic
    return resourceServerRead(d, m)
}

func resourceServerDelete(ctx context.Context, d *
schema.ResourceData, m interface {}) diag.Diagnostics {

    //implementation logic
    d.SetId("")

}
```

As we have used the context-aware functions, all four functions provide the same parameters; however, the *ResourceData means different things for different functions. *ResourceData is used to query and set the attributes of a resource. *ResourceData is the primary argument received for CRUD operations on a resource as well as configuration of a provider. It can be used to query data, and check for changes. The most relevant methods are Get and Set. Get returns the data for the given key, or nil if the key doesn't exist in the schema. If the key does exist in the schema but doesn't exist in the configuration, then the default value for that type will be returned. For strings, this default is "", for numbers it is 0, etc. If you want to test if something is set at all in the configuration, use GetOk. GetOk returns the data for the given key and whether or not the key has been set to a non-zero value at some point. GetChange returns the old and new value for a given key. HasChange should be used to check if a change exists. HasChange(key string) returns whether or not the given key has been changed. HasChanges(keys ...string) returns whether or not any of the given keys has been changed. Set(key string, value interface{}) sets the value for the given key. If the key is invalid or the value is not a correct type, an error will be returned. `State()` returns the new resource instance state after any `Set` calls. In order to build the final state attributes, read the full attribute set as a `map[string]interface{}`, write it to a `MapFieldWriter`, and then use that map.

First off, for this example the `interface{}` parameter will be `nil` because we did not define a `ConfigureFunc` in the Provider. This parameter is conventionally used to store API clients and other provider instance specific data.

4.8.1 Create Functionality

`CreateContext` is called automatically by Terraform when the provider must create a new instance of a managed resource. The `*ResourceData` parameter contains the plan and the saved state data for this managed resource instance. The available data in the `Get*` methods is the proposed state, which is the merged data of the runtime Terraform configuration and saved state data. For a brand new resource it has no saved state and all data comes from configuration. Typically, at the beginning of `CreateContext`, you would need to decode the data from the `*ResourceData` object into some local variables of corresponding struct types for making the API calls. In the `CreateContext` function itself, call the `SetId` method with a non-empty value for the managed resource instance to be properly saved into the Terraform state. The `resourceServerCreate()` function returns with a call to the `resourceServerRead()` function.

In our example provider, we could obtain the planned value for the resource's attributes, `environment_id` for a Platform.sh Environment, and call Platform.sh API Endpoint for the environment to initialize a new environment. As mentioned before, Platform.sh does not provide an API endpoint to create a brand new Environment resource. The API endpoint to initialize a new environment is https:// *ca-1* .platform.sh/api/projects/ *zis3mqzwuqnu4* /environments/ *environment_id* /initialize . The project id would be different for different developers, and so could the API region (ca-1 in example). You would use an instance of the go-resty client. The Accept and Content-Type headers need to be set in the client call. The Accept specifies the format of the response data and the Content-Type indicates to the server the format of the request data. Both these headers are set to `application/json`. The Golang library called json can be used to build/marshal and read/unmarshal JSON. The POST REST endpoint provided by the Platform.sh API means you have to use the `Post()` method. What the Platform.sh API expects in the request can be found from the API documentation for initialize .

The response object can be explored to get the details. An `environment_id` uniquely identifies an Environment resource in Platform.sh. Set its value in state with `setId()` supplying a non-null value. We don't want to set the id of the new resource that we just created with a null, or empty value. Because the `environmentId` of the resource we just created is not known as we are creating a new environment off an existing environment we may need to parse the response fields and get the value of the id of the new environment created. Some developers may find it easier to obtain some information such as the id of a new environment from the Platform.sh console and use it with their provider. The `resourceServerCreate()` function returns with a call to the `resourceServerRead()` function.

4.8.2 Read Functionality

`ReadContext` is called when the provider must refresh the state of a managed resource instance. The `ReadContext` function can be called automatically if needed by Terraform CLI commands that refresh state. After creating a new resource, the `resourceServerCreate()` function the provider developer needs to internally call the `ReadContext` field mapped function to set the new state. In the `ReadContext` field mapped function parameter list the `*ResourceData` parameter contains the state data for this managed resource instance. The provider's developer must specify the logic to refresh the resource's state in the `resourceServerRead()` function. First, get the environment id from state, which is set in the `resourceServerCreate()` function, with an `Id()` function call. Next, get the details of the Environment using an HTTP call to the Platform.sh API using the go-resty client with a `Get()` function call. Map the response body to resource schema attributes. A resource's state can be represented as a map of attributes. Managed resources can signal to Terraform that the managed resource instance no longer exists and potentially should be recreated by calling the `SetId` method with an empty string ("") parameter and without returning an error.

4.8.3 Update Functionality

`UpdateContext` is called automatically when the provider must update an instance of a managed resource. Implementation of `UpdateContext` is optional. If omitted, all Schema attributes must enable the `ForceNew` field and any Terraform configured changes by an end user that would have otherwise caused an update will instead destroy and recreate the resource compontent. The `*ResourceData` parameter contains the plan and state data for this managed resource instance. The available data in the `Get*` methods is the proposed state, which is the merged data of the prior state and new user configuration. The `GetChange*` and `HasChange*` methods can be used to determine if an update needs to be made. The available data for the `GetChange*` and `HasChange*` methods are the prior state and proposed state. In the `resourceServerUpdate()` use the go-resty client's `Patch()` method to update the remote Platform.sh resource using the API endpoint for Update . In the return statement call the `ReadContext` field mapped function `resourceServerRead()` to refresh state with the updated infrastructure resource.

4.8.4 Delete Functionality

`DeleteContext` is called when the provider must delete, or destroy, the instance of a managed resource. The `*ResourceData` parameter contains the state data for this managed resource instance. In the `resourceServerDelete()` function Set the id of the resource in the state to an empty string to indicate to Terraform that the resource no longer exists. Terraform has no way of confirming any values we set in state explicitly, whether they accurately represent an infrastructure resource.

Authentication in each of the CRUD functions is handled with Platform.sh access tokens. The go-resty client method `SetAuthToken()` can be used to set an authentication token.

4.9 Error handling and logging

Error handling and logging are built into the Terraform plugin SDK. If error is a non-nil value it can be logged. Diagnostics report errors or warnings related to configuring the provider. All the functions (`CreateContext` , `ReadContext` , `UpdateContext` , and `DeleteContext`) that we use to serve a provider's functionality have return type as `diag.Diagnostics` , which can be used to return multiple errors and warnings to Terraform. This exposes diagnostics support when creating, reading, updating, deleting resources. An empty `diag.Diagnostics` slice indicates success, with no warnings or errors generated. The most common use case in Go will be handling a single error returned from a function. `FromErr` can be used to convert a Go error into a `Diagnostics`. As Go-resty is making the actual client calls to the Platform.sh API it is providing the initial error handling.

```
resp, err := client.R()...Post("...")
```

We need to convert a Go error to Terraform provider's `Diagnostic` using the `FromErr` as follows:

```
if err != nil {
    // Convert a Go error to Diagnostics
```

```
    return diag.FromErr(err)
}
```

`Diagnostics` is a collection of Warnings or Errors, and these can be collected in a slice type variable.

```
var diags diag.Diagnostics
```

Typically, we may append and build the list of diagnostics up until a fatal error is reached, which is when you should return the `Diagnostics` to the SDK. Conditionally add warning messages to `diags` using `diag.Diagnostic` instance/s. Diagnostic is a contextual message intended at outlining problems in user configuration. It supports multiple levels of severity (Error or Warning), a short Summary of the problem, an optional longer Detail message that can assist the user in fixing the problem, as well as an `AttributePath` representation which Terraform uses to indicate where the issue took place in the user's configuration. A `Diagnostic` will typically be used to pinpoint a problem with user configuration, however it can still be used to present warnings or errors to the user.

```
if someCondition {
    diags = append(diags, diag.Diagnostic {
        Severity: diag.Warning,
        Summary: "Warning level message",
        Detail: "Warning detail",
    })
}
```

We can return formatted error using helper method `Errorf` , which creates a `Diagnostics` with a single `Error` level `Diagnostic` entry formatted with `fmt.Sprintf` . This returns a single error in a `Diagnostics` as errors typically do not occur in multiples as warnings may.

```
if err != nil {
    diags = append(diags, diag.Errorf("unexpected: %s",
err)...) return diags
}
```

The `HasError` helper returns `true` if `Diagnostics` contains an instance of `Severity == Error`. This helper is similar to error handling in Go with `if err != nil{}`.

Use logging for debugging or informational purposes. The SDKs used for developing a Provider/Plugin; terraform-plugin-framework, and terraform-plugin-sdk/v2 provide built-in support for logging. Log output can be set at varying verbosity levels - Error, Warn, Info, Debug, Trace. Use the `tflog` package to write logs for your provider. All calls to `tflog` package functionality must use an SDK provided `context.Context`, which stores the logging implementation. Every terraform-plugin-framework method implemented by providers automatically includes the correct `context.Context`. Providers written with terraform-plugin-sdk must use context-aware functionality, such as the `helper/schema.Resource` type `ReadContext` field. Example of logging:

```
client := resty.New()
tflog.Info(ctx, "Using Platform.sh API token for
authentication")
```

The `resource_server.go` is listed:

```go
package main

import (
        "fmt"
        "context"

        "github.com/go-resty/resty/v2"
        "github.com/hashicorp/terraform-plugin-
sdk/v2/helper/schema"
        "github.com/hashicorp/terraform-plugin-sdk/v2/diag"
        "github.com/hashicorp/terraform-plugin-log/tflog"
)

func resourceServer() *schema.Resource {
        return &schema.Resource{
                CreateContext: resourceServerCreate,
                ReadContext:   resourceServerRead,
                UpdateContext: resourceServerUpdate,
                DeleteContext: resourceServerDelete,

                Schema: map[string]*schema.Schema{
                        "environment_id": &schema.Schema{
                                Type:     schema.TypeString,
                                Required: true,
                        },
                        "name": &schema.Schema{
                                Type:     schema.TypeString,
                                Optional: true,
                                Default:  "a platform env",
                        },
                },
        }
}

func resourceServerCreate(ctx context.Context, d
*schema.ResourceData, m interface{}) diag.Diagnostics   {
        environment_id := d.Get("environment_id").(string)

        client := resty.New()
```

```go
        tflog.Info(ctx, "Using Platform.sh API token for
authentication")
        resp, err := client.R().SetHeader("Accept",
"application/json").SetHeader("Content-Type",
"application/json").SetBody("{'repository':
'git@github.com:Deepak-Vohra/greetings.git@master','profile':
'Greetings Project','files': [{'mode': 0600,'path':
'config.json','contents':
'{}'}]}").SetAuthToken("eyJhbGciOi").Post("https://ca-
1.platform.sh/api/projects/zis3mqzwuqnu4/environments/" +
environment_id + "/initialize")
        if err != nil {
            // Convert a Go error to Diagnostics
            return diag.FromErr(err)
        }

    // Explore response object (optional)
    fmt.Println("Response Info:")
    fmt.Println("  Error       :", err)
    fmt.Println("  Status Code:", resp.StatusCode())
    fmt.Println("  Status      :", resp.Status())
    fmt.Println("  Proto       :", resp.Proto())
    fmt.Println("  Time        :", resp.Time())
    fmt.Println("  Received At:", resp.ReceivedAt())
    fmt.Println("  Body        :\n", resp)
    fmt.Println()

    //Obtain id of new environment from the response Body and
set in the resource's state
    d.SetId("new environment id")

    return resourceServerRead(ctx, d, m)
}

func resourceServerRead(ctx context.Context, d
*schema.ResourceData, m interface{}) diag.Diagnostics  {
    environment_id := d.Id()
    client := resty.New()
    resp, err := client.R().SetHeader("Accept",
"application/json").SetAuthToken("eyJhbGciOiJFUzI").Get("https://
ca-1.platform.sh/api/projects/zis3mqzwuqnu4/environments/" +
environment_id)

    // Collect Errors & Warnings in a slice type
  var diags diag.Diagnostics
    // Return formatted error
    if err != nil {
        diags = append(diags, diag.Errorf("unexpected: %s",
err)...)
        return diags
    }
```

```go
        // Explore response object (optional)
        fmt.Println("Response Info:")
        fmt.Println("  Error       :", err)
        fmt.Println("  Status Code:", resp.StatusCode())
        fmt.Println("  Status      :", resp.Status())
        fmt.Println("  Proto       :", resp.Proto())
        fmt.Println("  Time        :", resp.Time())
        fmt.Println("  Received At:", resp.ReceivedAt())
        fmt.Println("  Body        :\n", resp)
        fmt.Println()

        //  Map the response body to resource schema attributes
        // Update state
        return nil
}

func resourceServerUpdate(ctx context.Context, d
*schema.ResourceData, m interface{}) diag.Diagnostics  {
        //Implementation is optional
        environment_id := d.Get("environment_id").(string) //unique
resource identifier
        //name := d.Get("name").(string)

        client := resty.New()
        resp, err := client.R().SetHeader("Accept",
"application/json").SetHeader("Content-Type",
"application/json").SetBody("{'name': 'updated env','title':
'updated
env'}").SetAuthToken("eyJhbGciOiJFUzI").Patch("https://ca-
1.platform.sh/api/projects/zis3mqzwuqnu4/environments/" +
environment_id)
        if err != nil {
            // Convert a Go error to Diagnostics
             return diag.FromErr(err)
            }

        // Explore response object

        //Call Read to update state with the updated resource
        return resourceServerRead(ctx, d, m)
}

func resourceServerDelete(ctx context.Context, d
*schema.ResourceData, m interface{}) diag.Diagnostics  {
        environment_id := d.Id()

        d.SetId("")
        client := resty.New()
        resp, err := client.R().SetHeader("Accept",
"application/json").SetAuthToken("eyJhbGciOi").Delete("https://ca
```

```
-1.platform.sh/api/projects/zis3mqzwuqnu4/environments/" +
environment_id)
    if err != nil {
        // Convert a Go error to Diagnostics
        return diag.FromErr(err)
    }

    // Explore response object
        return nil
}
```

4.10 Compiling the Golang Source Code to Binaries

First run the go mod tidy command to load all the required packages including
dependencies. The command ensures that all the go modules required by the main
module are listed in the go.mod file with a require directive. Partial output from the
command lists downloading the go-resty module:

```
$ go mod tidy
go: finding module for package github.com/go-resty/resty/v2
go: downloading github.com/go-resty/resty/v2 v2.13.1
go: downloading github.com/go-resty/resty v1.12.0
go: found github.com/go-resty/resty/v2 in github.com/go-
resty/resty/v2 v2.13.1
```

Having downloaded all the requisite modules/packages, build the Provider Golang source
code. Build the Provider Golang source code using the go build command in which
the - o flag specifies the output binaries file name. If the command returns without any
message it means the binaries have been built successfully.

```
:~/terraform-provider-example$ go build -o terraform-
provider-example
```

A terraform-provider-example binaries get created in the same directory.
Create a directory structure in the ~/.terraform.d/plugins directory for the
compiled binaries so that Terraform can find them.

```
mkdir -p ~/.terraform.d/plugins/terraform-
example.com/exampleprovider/example/1 .0.0/linux_amd64
```

Copy the compiled binaries to the directory you just created.

```
~/terraform-provider-example$ cp terraform-provider-example
~/.terraform.d/plugins/terraform-
example.com/exampleprovider/example/1 .0.0/linux_amd64
```

Remember to delete the binaries from the ~/.terraform.d/plugin-cache directory if you recompile the binaries.

```
cd ~/.terraform.d/plugin-cache
:~/.terraform.d/plugin-cache$ ls -l
drwxr-xr-x 3 deepakvohra deepakvohra 4096 May 25 22:42
terraform-example.com
:~/.terraform.d/plugin-cache$ rm -r terraform-example.com
```

4.11 Summary

We started this chapter introducing the different provider development approaches, followed by prerequisite setup. To develop a new Terraform provider, we initialized a Golang module. Subsequently, we created a Terraform provider schema. We created a resource schema. We also need to configure in the go-resty client. We created the Create, Read, Update, and Delete resource action functions. We discussed error handling and logging, and finally compiled the Golang source code to binaries.

In the next chapter, we configure and use a Terraform CLI.

5. Terraform CLI

In this chapter we configure and use a Terraform CLI (command line interface). This chapter has the following sections:

- Configuring Terraform CLI
- Using Terraform CLI

5.1 Configuring Terraform CLI

A Terraform module consists of configuration files (`.tf` and `.tf.json`) in a single working directory. Terraform configuration language doesn't require any file naming conventions, or a fixed number of `.tf` files. You may want to take advantage of this flexibility to use multiple `.tf` files, one for each purpose such as `variables.tf`, `versions.tf`, `outputs.tf` and such. At the minimum create a `main.tf` file to configure a resource with a resource block. These files can be named as a user deems suitable as long as the configuration blocks within them describe distinct objects. Terraform uses all the configuration files together and returns an error if two configuration blocks describe the same object. Create a working directory for the root module.

5.2 Creating Terraform Configuration Files

Next, we shall use the Terraform CLI to initialize a working directory, plan a resource create/update, and apply a resource create/update. Create a `main.tf` in the working directory and copy following configuration to it:

```
resource "example_server" "my-server-name" {
    provider = example environment_id ="branch_of_main"
}
```

The resource type is specified as `example_server`, which is the same as configured in the provider resources map in `provider.go`. The `my-server-name` is the local name for the resource and has context only within the module. The resource's arguments are specified in `{}`. We set two resource attributes in `resource_server.go`: `environment_id` and `name`. All required resource attributes must be specified in the `resource{}` block. In the example provider `environment_id` is the only required resource attribute. The `main.tf` specifies the `provider` meta-argument. Terraform Configuration Language supports some optional meta-arguments to be specified with any resource type. These meta-arguments are:

- depends_on - To specify hidden dependencies
- count - To create multiple resource instances according to a count
- for_each - To create multiple instances according to a map, or set of strings
- provider - To explicitly select a non-default provider configuration.

By default Terraform selects a provider based on the resource type.

- lifecycle - To customize lifecycle
- provisioner - To configure post-creation extra actions

Create a second .tf file called versions.tf to configure the required providers including their version constraints if any, and source. Each module must declare the required providers with the required_providers block. Our example versions.tf declares the example provider. The source is a global source address from which the provider can be downloaded and is in the format [<HOSTNAME>/]<NAMESPACE>/<TYPE>. The <HOSTNAME> defaults to registry.terraform.io if omitted. The <NAMESPACE> is the organizational namespace and is unique on a host. The <TYPE> is the short name for the provider and must be unique within the host/namespace. The required_version within the terraform {} block is a version requirement for Terraform itself. The versions.tf also includes a provider configuration. Provider configuration can specify the provider's remote API, region, endpoint URL, or other requirements such as username and password. The meta-argument alias can be used to specify an alternate configuration for the provider. Or the provider configuration block can be empty. Terraform could output a message requiring a provider block, even if it is to be empty. The versions.tf is listed:

```
terraform{
    required_providers{
        example ={
            version ="">= 1.0.0"
            source ="terraform-
example.com/exampleprovider/example"
        }
    }
    required_version ="">= 1.1.0"
}

provider "example"{
    # ...
}
```

Our Terraform module working directory has only two .tf files:

```
deepakvohra@localhost:~/terraform-provider-
example/terraform$ ls -l
```

```
-rw-rw-r-- main.tf
-rw-rw-r-- versions.tf
```

Next, we use the Terraform Provider we just created using a local Terraform configuration.

5.3 Using Terraform CLI

Having compiled the provider, we are ready to take it for a test spin. As the scope of this short book does not include hosting the provider, we won't actually be making calls to the Platform.sh API endpoints. But we do take the resource through a cycle of initialization, create, update, and delete. To start with, it is important to understand when each of the Create/Read/Update/Delete action functions are called automatically by Terraform. Based on the Terraform configuration provided in `main.tf` and `versions.tf`, and the present state of a resource Terraform automatically determines whether to create/update/delete a resource by making a corresponding action function call. The illustration in Figure 5.1 explains how Terraform determines whether to create/update/delete a resource. The Terraform calls the Read function to refresh the state of a resource each time the terraform plan and terraform apply are called. The refreshed state is only kept in memory by default and it is to ensure that the changes Terraform recommends/plans or actually tries to apply are aware of the actual state of the resource.

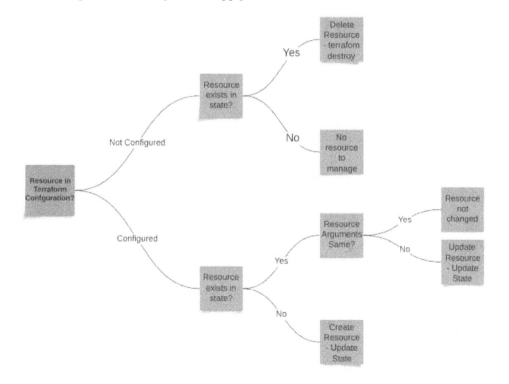

Figure 5.1. How Terraform Determines which function to call

As an example path in the illustration, the Terraform configuration specifies a resource, such as the `example_server` resource in our `main.tf`. And, the resource does not exist in the state file. Terraform creates a new resource using the configuration provided when `terraform apply` is run.

As another example, Terraform resource configuration specifies a resource and the resource state also exists in the cached state file. When `terraform apply` is run, the resource is updated to match what is configured in the configuration file. As a third example, a resource is not set in the configuration file, which would be setting the `environment_id` resource attribute to an empty string, but the resource has a state in the cached state file. The resource gets deleted when `terraform destroy` is run.

First, run `terraform init` to initialize a working directory, which contains the Terraform configuration files. The `init` command downloads and installs all the required providers. The output is listed:

```
deepakvohra@localhost:~/terraform-provider-
example/terraform$ terraform init
Initializing the backend...
Initializing provider plugins...
        -  Finding terraform-
           example.com/exampleprovider/example versions
           matching ">= 1.0.0"...
        -  - Installing terraform-
           example.com/exampleprovider/example v1.0.0...
        -  - Installed terraform-
           example.com/exampleprovider/example v1.0.0
           (unauthenticated) Terraform has created a lock
           file .terraform.lock.hcl to record the provider
           selections it made above. Include this file in
           your version control repository so that Terraform
           can guarantee to make the same selections by
           default when you run "terraform init" in the
           future. Terraform has been successfully
           initialized!
        -
You may now begin working with Terraform. Try running
"terraform plan" to see any changes that are required for
your infrastructure. All Terraform commands should now
work. If you ever set or change modules or backend
configuration for Terraform, rerun this command to
reinitialize your working directory. If you forget, other
commands will detect it and remind you to do so if
necessary.
```

We should run the `terraform validate` command to validate the configuration files.

```
deepakvohra@localhost:~/terraform-provider-
example/terraform$ terraform validate Success! The
configuration is valid.
```

Next, run the `terraform plan` command to create a run plan that you can preview. The output indicates that a resource called `example_server.my-server-name` will be created.

```
deepakvohra@localhost:~/terraform-provider-
example/terraform$ terraform plan Terraform used the
selected providers to generate the following execution
plan. Resource actions are indicated with the following
symbols:

+ create Terraform will perform the following actions: #
example_server.my-server-name will be created
+ resource "example_server" "my-server-name" { +
environment_id = "backup_of_main" + id = (known after
apply) + name = "a platform env" }
Plan: 1 to add, 0 to change, 0 to destroy.

Note: You didn't use the -out option to save this plan, so
Terraform can't guarantee to take exactly these actions if
you run "terraform apply" now.
```

Finally, run the `terraform apply` command to create the resource. This time you are prompted for acknowledgement before actually creating a resource.

```
deepakvohra@localhost:~/terraform-provider-
example/terraform$ terraform apply Terraform used the
selected providers to generate the following execution
plan. Resource actions are indicated with the following
symbols:
+ create Terraform will perform the following actions: #
example_server.my-server-name will be created
+ resource "example_server" "my-server-name" {
+ environment_id = "backup_of_main"
+ id = (known after apply) + name = "a platform env" }

Plan: 1 to add, 0 to change, 0 to destroy. Do you want to
perform these actions? Terraform will perform the actions
described above. Only 'yes' will be accepted to approve.
Enter a value: yes
example_server.my-server-name: Creating...
```

```
example_server.my-server-name: Creation complete after 1s
[id=new environment id] Apply complete! Resources: 1 added,
0 changed, 0 destroyed.
```

To update the resource created, update the `main.tf` as follows:

```
resource "example_server" "my-server-name"{
    provider ="example"
    environment_id ="branch-of-main"
    name = "main env"
}
```

Run `teraform validate` and `terraform plan` again with the following output.

deepakvohra@localhost:~/terraform-provider-example/terraform$ terraform validate
Success! The configuration is valid.

```
deepakvohra@localhost:~/terraform-provider-
example/terraform$ terraform plan example_server.my-server-
name: Refreshing state... [id=new environment id] Terraform
used the selected providers to generate the following
execution plan. Resource actions are indicated with the
following symbols: ~ update in-place Terraform will perform
the following actions:
# example_server.my-server-name will be updated in-place ~
resource "example_server" "my-server-name" { id = "new
environment id" ~ name = "a platform env" -> "updated env"
# (1 unchanged attribute hidden) }
Plan: 0 to add, 1 to change, 0 to destroy. Note: You didn't
use the -out option to save this plan, so Terraform can't
guarantee to take exactly these actions if you run
"terraform apply" now.
```

Run `terraform apply` again with the following output:

```
deepakvohra@localhost:~/terraform-provider-
example/terraform$ terraform apply example_server.my-
server-name: Refreshing state... [id=new environment id]
Terraform used the selected providers to generate the
following execution plan. Resource actions are indicated
with the following symbols: ~ update in-place Terraform
will perform the following actions:
# example_server.my-server-name will be updated in-place ~
resource "example_server" "my-server-name" { id = "new
environment id" ~ name = "a platform env" -> "updated env"
# (1 unchanged attribute hidden) } Plan: 0 to add, 1 to
change, 0 to destroy. Do you want to perform these actions?
```

Terraform will perform the actions described above. Only
'yes' will be accepted to approve.
Enter a value: yes
example_server.my-server-name: Modifying... [id=new
environment id] example_server.my-server-name:
Modifications complete after 0s [id=new environment id]
Apply complete! Resources: 0 added, 1 changed, 0 destroyed.

To delete the resource modify the main.tf as follows to set environment_id to an
empty string.

```
resource "example_server" "my-server-name"{
    provider ="example"
    environment_id = ""
    name = "updated env"
}
```

Run the terraform destroy command. You are prompted and select yes. The
output indicates that the resource is deleted.

```
deepakvohra@localhost:~/terraform-provider-
example/terraform$ terraform destroy example_server.my-
server-name: Refreshing state... [id=new environment id]
Terraform used the selected providers to generate the
following execution plan. Resource actions are indicated
with the following symbols: - destroy Terraform will
perform the following actions:
# example_server.my-server-name will be destroyed -
resource "example_server" "my-server-name" { -
environment_id = "backup_of_main" -> null - id = "new
environment id" -> null - name = "updated env" -> null }
Plan: 0 to add, 0 to change, 1 to destroy.
Do you really want to destroy all resources?
Terraform will destroy all your managed infrastructure, as
shown above.
There is no undo. Only 'yes' will be accepted to confirm.
Enter a value: yes
example_server.my-server-name: Destroying... [id=new
environment id] example_server.my-server-name: Destruction
complete after 0s Destroy complete! Resources: 1 destroyed.
```

Note: We have used a placeholder example provider with a placeholder hostname. For a
production-ready provider you would need to provide an actual hostname. An example
placeholder host terraform-example.com could generate error message such as the
following:

49

```
Terraform failed to fetch the requested providers for
linux_amd64 in order to calculate their checksums: some
providers could not be installed: - terraform-
example.com/exampleprovider/example: could not connect to
terraform-example.com: failed to request discovery
document: Get "https://terraform-example.com/.well-
known/terraform.json": dial tcp: lookup terraform-
example.com on 127.0.0.53:53: no such host.
```

5.4 Summary

In this chapter we created a Terraform configuration files. We introduced how Terraform determines which CRUD functionality to invoke. Subsequently, we used Terraform CLI with the example Terraform Provider.

6. Terraform Provider Best Practices

Next, We discuss some real-world considerations for building production-ready providers.

The best practices for Terraform providers are described in Figure 6.1.

Development	Style & Structure	Testing & Hosting	Documentation	Security	Versioning & Publishing
Golang + Terraform HCL	Naming Conventions	Unit tests	Schema Attributes	Dynamic Credentials	Provider registry protocol
Single Responsibility Principle	Terraform Formatting	Integration tests	Functionality to manage a Resource (Resource's API)	API Tokens (per Platform.sh Organization)	Module registry (reusable modules)
Self-contained Functions	Standard Module Layout	Mocks	Auto-generated documentation (tfplugindocs)	Expirable OAuth2 Access Tokens	Terraform registry (open source modules)
Resource Schema matches Resource API	Variables' usage interpretable	Use Hostname/ Namespace/ type format	Example Usage	Sensitive Attributes & Input Variables	Private registry (private modules)
Resources importable	Outputs Usable	Configure Supported Platforms	Arguments Reference	HashiCorp Vault for Storage	Up-to-date
Delete binaries from plugin cache after recompiling		Don't upload .tfstate, .terraform and other development-related files			State Continuity
Well Managed Provider Dependencies	Scripts - avoid			Masking Sensitive Output	Semantic Versioning 2.0.0

Figure 6.1. Best Practices

Next, We briefly go over some of these.

6.1 Development

The Single Responsibility Principle recommends that a single provider should serve resource/s from a single underlying API. You would create a single provider for a REST API and serve the different PaaS resources the API has endpoints for, such as project, and environment. It is not recommended to combine multiple API resources in a single provider. A single resource definition should represent a single API resource. For example, one resource definition for a Platform.sh project, and a separate resource definition for a Platform.sh environment. It is easier to develop, maintain, and use a provider that takes into consideration the single responsibility principle.

A Terraform resource schema should match the naming and structure of the resource API it represents with due consideration for Provider naming conventions. As an example, the Platform.sh Environment resource API identifies a single environment by its environmentId. We used the attribute name as `environment_id`, which closely matches the resource API. We can't use attribute name as `environmentId` because Terraform provider naming recommends "Attribute names within Terraform configuration blocks are conventionally named as all-lowercase with underscores separating words..". It is not just a recommendation but an error message is output if we used environmentId as attribute name.

The action functions (CRUD) in a provider should each perform a single computation only and not use conditional logic to put all computation into one function. The provider's functions should have predictable functionality. In other words, the functions are self-contained and their output is not influenced by environment settings, network settings, or other parameters that could change over time.

Provider typically depends on other providers and the dependencies should be well managed so that the required provider versions are downloaded. A required provider configured in Terraform configuration can specify version constraints. The `.terraform.lock.hcl` dependency lock file can be used to track provider dependencies. Terraform creates the file in the working directory, which is the directory with all the `.tf` files, when you run `terraform init` to initialize.

If you recompile provider golang binaries during development, remember to delete the cached binaries from the `$HOME/.terraform.d/plugin-cache` directory, which you may remember setting as the value for the environment variable `plugin_cache_dir`, before your next run of Terraform configuration. Terraform makes use of provider checksum verification and the checksum are recorded in the dependency lock file. If you update provider version and run it for the first time you could get a messages such as:

```
Error while installing terraform-
example.com/exampleprovider/example v1.0.0:the local
package for terraform-example.com/exampleprovider/example
1.0.0 doesn't match any of the checksums previously
recorded in the dependency lock file (this might be because
the available checksums are for packages targeting
different platforms); for more information:
https://www.terraform.io/language/provider-checksum-
verification
```

6.2 Style & Structure

In naming Terraform resources and resource attributes lowercase and underscores are the norm. Take advantage of the flexibility both Golang and Terraform provide in naming files within a modular structure, and name the fields to represent groupings. The different Golang source code files within the same package name could be named to indicate their purpose. As an example, the `provider.go` could describe the provider's schema, and a resource_server.go file could describe a resource's schema including functions for CRUD actions on the resource API. Similarly, a Terraform configuration could be divided into multiple .tf files, with each .tf representing an aspect of the configuration, such as main.tf, versions.tf, variables.tf. Variables should be configured in an interpretable way. A variable's name should suggest its purpose, project_region as an example. Outputs may need to be consumed, therefore expose output values. Output values should reference resources' attributes instead of input variables. Referencing resource attributes is the recommended approach because it enables Terraform to describe dependencies when one module refers to output values from another module. Terraform files should pass the formatting expected by the terraform fmt command, which can be used to rewrite configuration files to the Terraform configuration style conventions. Scripts should be avoided to create resources directly because the state of the resources created by custom scripts is not managed by Terraform. Helper scripts, if any, should be put into a separate directory.

6.3 Testing and Hosting

Terraform provides a testing framework in v1.6.0 and later. Integration and unit tests run with the terraform test command let you test your Terraform configurations without introducing breaking changes or changing the state of a resource. These tests do test real resources; however, the tests create only minimal needed resources and for a short time only. Unit tests test a unit of code such as a class, a function, or an endpoint. Integration tests test the interaction between the different units of code to ensure that they integrate seamlessly.

As of Terraform version 1.7.0 mocks can be created for providers, resources, and data sources. Mocks use fake data and don't actually access a resource, or even need access credentials. The terraform test takes test files (.tftest.hcl or .tftest.json) as parameters to run the tests specified within the run blocks of the test files. The command attribute within a run block configures whether to run a complete apply operation, which is the default and suitable for integration testing as it creates a real resource, albeit for a short time only. If you want to run unit tests to validate logic operations without actually creating a resource, set command = plan in the test file.

Testify is a toolkit for running unit tests for Golang, and if your Golang module requires it, it gets downloaded when you run go mod tidy. Bash Automated Testing System (BATS) can be used to test Golang modules running in a test harness. A test harness is a testing system that is suitable for integration testing as it provides all that is needed in the form of stubs, test data, and drivers, and generates reports for the test results. BATS supports the Test Anything Protocol (TAP) protocol, which makes use of producers and consumers. The tap-go package can be used to produce TAP output.

If you work with different platforms (OS+architecture) you should consider updating the .terraform.lock.hcl file with a platform that you may use by calling the `terraform providers lock` command with the `-platform=OS_ARCH` argument. If you use a different platform that has not been configured, you could get a messages such as:

```
The current .terraform.lock.hcl file only includes
checksums for linux_amd64,so Terraform running on another
platform will fail to install these providers. To calculate
additional checksums for another platform, run: terraform
providers lock -platform=linux_amd64 (where linux_amd64 is
the platform to generate)
```

A provider must have an address in the format *hostname/namespace/type*, where *hostname* is the registry host and defaults to `registry.terraform.io`. Any provider not hosted on `registry.terraform.io` is a third-party provider. The *namespace* should be unique on a hostname. It could be the name of the organization that is packaging and distributing the provider. The provider *type* must be unique within a hostname/namespace. The provider type can be almost any arbitrary name such as "aws", "platform". The Terraform configuration will output an error message if any validation issue is found.

We are likely to get the following error message if we used type as "terraform-provider-platform":

```
Error: Invalid provider type on versions.tf line 5, in
terraform Provider source ".../terraform-provider-platform"
has a type with the prefix "terraform-provider-", which
isn't valid. Although that prefix is often used in the
names of version control repositories for Terraform
providers, provider source strings should not include it.
```

6.4 Documentation

The documentation for your provider should include example usage. We defined our schema attributes when we built the provider, and we must list and discuss the schema attributes in the documentation. Documentation must include an arguments reference that provides a detailed syntax of using the various resource arguments and what resource they are associated with. It must discuss the functionality provided by the provider, such as create, read, update,and delete of a resource. The Resource API endpoint/s that a provider serves must be included. Use the tfplugindocs command to generate documentation automatically. Because the command is a
Terraform command the documentation is generated in a format that the Terraform registry supports. It provides three subcommands to perform the corresponding action for documentation : generate, validate, migrate.

6.5 Security

If you remember from earlier discussion, we generated an API Token in Platform.sh and used this token to generate an access token (oauth2). This access token is a user's access credentials and must be used and stored securely. Terraform configuration supports marking an input variable, and a resource argument with the sensitive attribute to indicate that the variable/resource attribute contains confidential information. Input variables are like function arguments and you would make a variable sensitive as in the following example:

```
variable "access_token" { type = object({ name = string api
= string }) sensitive = true description = "The access
token to access Platform.sh API" }
```

When you run terrform plan and terraform apply, the sensitive variable's value will not be shown in the output. Any resource that references a sensitive variable is also considered sensitive and its value is not shown in the terraform CLI output. The following resource references a sensitive variable access_token:

```
resource "example_server" "example_server_1" { name =
var.access_token.name address = var.access_token.api }
```

Sensitive information (resource_id, password, access_token) is stored as such without any obfuscation in the resource state (.tfstate file), and therefore the resource state must be considered sensitive information as well. Storing state remotely can be used to alleviate the risk of making sensitive information available from a user's local state file. For persistent storage of sensitive information including login credentials the HashiCorp Vault can be used. And the information can be injected into Terraform configuration using the Vault provider . Sensitive information that is likely to change such as login credentials is best managed with a set of best practices:

1. Create a separate variables_sensitive.tf file for sensitive variables
2. Reference the sensitive variables in the main.tf file
3. Create a variable definition .tfvars file to provide current values for the sensitive variables
4. Apply the .tfvars file with the -var-file command line parameter to terraform plan, and terraform apply

Expressions used in output values can reference sensitive values only if the sensitive attribute for the output in outputs.tf is set to true. The output won't actually output the sensitive value but instead indicate that the value is sensitive, as example:

```
user_name = <sensitive>
```

Presently, providers do not omit/obfuscate sensitive information from error log messages. If an error message includes a sensitive variable or resource argument it is logged as such. One alternative is to treat the error logs as sensitive information. Another option that could alleviate the issue of sensitive data getting logged in error messages is to reduce the verbosity of logs in the TF_LOG environment variable. From high to low verbosity the settings are : TRACE, DEBUG, INFO, WARN or ERROR.

6.6 Versioning & Publishing

A provider must be up-to-date with the resource API that it serves. To maintain state continuity versioning of provider releases must be performed and documented. The version numbering scheme must follow the Semantic Versioning 2.0.0 . A provider/module can be published to a registry to share it within an organization, or for public use. A published provider must follow the Provider registry protocol . A provider can be published to one of the supported registry types:

- Module registry (reusable modules)
- Terraform registry (open source modules)
- Private registry (private modules)

6.7 Summary

In this chapter we discussed some best practices to follow for Terraform provider development. This chapter concludes this short book.

7. Afterword

In this book, we introduced you to Terraform Providers and their benefits in streamlining your IaC (Infrastructure as Code) workflow. Terraform Providers are abstractions that expose upstream resources that make REST API endpoints available to manage the resources. Terraform is used for infrastructure automation and infrastructure doesn't have to be an IaaS (Infrastructure as a Service) such as a VM compute instance, VPC, or load balancer. It can be a PaaS (Platform as a Service) such as the one provided by Platform.sh. You need only three Terraform components to build and use a Terraform Provider : a Terraform Plugin SDK/Platform, Terraform configuration language files, and Terraform command line interface. You learned how to use Terraform Plugin SDK V2 to build an example Terraform Provider to perform CRUD operations on a PaaS resource - environment in Platform.sh. Subsequently, you learned how to use terraform init, terraform plan, and terraform apply to initialize, plan, and apply an example Terraform configuration using the example provider. You learned about the best practices in developing a Terraform Provider. You learned about best practices relating to naming conventions, development, testing, hosting, sensitive information handling, documentation, and versioning & publishing.

INDEX

API endpoints, 23
API token, 11
authentication, 11
AWS CloudFormation, 25
Bash Automated Testing System, 53
best practices, 51
binaries, 40
configuration files, 43
CRUD, 2, 8, 30
data source, 8
data structures, 6
Diagnostics, 35
error handling, 35
go.mod file, 6
Golang, 5
  install, 25
  module, 26
Golang-HashiCorp Configuration
  Language, 25
Go-resty, 30
Infrastructure as Code, 1
logging, 35
managed resource, 8

mocks, 53
plugins, 1
provider entrypoint, 28
resource, 6
resource action functions, 30
resource lifecycle, 9
resource schema, 28
RESTful API, 1
schema, 6, 27
Semantic Versioning, 56
Single Responsibility Principle, 51
Terraform
  install, 25
Terraform CLI, 43
Terraform Configuration Language, 1
Terraform Plugin Framework, 6
Terraform Plugin SDK v2, 6
Terraform Plugins, 5
Terraform Providers, 1
  components, 5, 10, 57
  structure, 6
Terraform Registry, 2
unit tests, 53

www.ingramcontent.com/pod-product-compliance
Lightning Source LLC
LaVergne TN
LVHW051613050326
832903LV00033B/4473